LIVES
AND
TIMES

Susan B. Anthony

Peter and Connie Roop

Heinemann Library
Chicago, Illinois

© 1998 Reed Educational & Professional Publishing
Published by Heinemann Interactive Library,
an imprint of Reed Educational & Professional Publishing,
Chicago, IL

Customer Service 888-454-2279

Visit our website at www.heinemannlibrary.com

Printed in Hong Kong / China
Designed by Ken Vail Graphic Design, Cambridge.
Illustrations by Deborah Kindred (Linden Artist)

02 01
10 9 8 7 6 5 4 3

Library of Congress Cataloging-in-Publication data

Roop, Peter.
    Susan B. Anthony / Peter and Connie Roop.
        p.   cm. -- (Lives & times)
    Includes bibliographical references and index.
    Summary: An introductory biography of the early feminist who
fought for women's right to vote.
    ISBN 1-57572-563-0 (lib. bdg.)
    1. Anthony, Susan B. (Susan Brownell), 1820-1906 -- Juvenile
literature. 2. Feminists -- United States -- Biography -- Juvenile
literature. 3. Suffragists -- United States -- Biography -- Juvenile
literature. (1. Anthony. Susan B. (Susan Brownell), 1820-1906.
2. Feminists. 3. Women Biography.) I. Roop, Connie. II. Title.
III. Series: Lives and times (Crystal Lake, Ill.)
HQ1413.A55R66 1997
305. 42' 092 dc21
    (B)   97-13731
                                                       CIP
                                                       AC

Some words are shown in bold, **like this**.
You can find out what they mean by looking in the
glossary. The glossary also helps you say difficult
words.

Acknowledgements
The author and publishers are grateful to the following for permission to reproduce copyright
photographs:
Corbis-Bethman, pp.18,20; Corbis-Bethmann/UPI, p.22
Culver Pictures Inc, pp. 16, 17; Martin, Phil, pp. 19, 21, 23

Cover photograph: Culver Pictures Inc

Special thanks to Betty Root for her comments in the preparation of this book.

Every effort has been made to contact copyright holders of any material reproduced in this
book. Any omissions will be rectified in subsequent printings if notice is given to the publisher.

Contents

Part One

Susan Brownell Anthony was born on February 15, 1820, in Adams, Massachusetts. She was the second of the eight children in her family. Her father ran a **weaving mill**.

Susan's father raised his children in the **Quaker** religion. One Quaker belief is that women are **equal** to men. At the time, many people did not believe this.

When Susan was young, people believed a woman's place was at home, cooking, cleaning, and raising children. Teaching was one of the few jobs women could do.

Susan was a teacher for fifteen years. She earned $2.50 a week. Susan was unhappy that men were paid four times more for doing the same job.

In 1851, Susan met Elizabeth Cady Stanton.
Stanton was one of the leaders of the new
women's rights movement. Over the
next fifty years they led the fight for
women's rights.

During the **Civil War** (1861–1865), Susan and Elizabeth worked to gain freedom for **slaves**. With their help, a **law** was passed after the war that freed all slaves.

One of Susan's and Elizabeth's goals was to get **property** rights for women. One **law** said everything a woman owned really belonged to her husband or father.

In 1866, this unfair **law** was changed so women could keep their money and property. This was one small step toward **equality** between women and men.

In all but two states, only men were allowed to **vote**. Susan believed that the **United States Constitution** also promised every woman the right to vote.

On **Election Day** in 1872, Susan voted!
It was still against the **law** for a woman to
vote. She got arrested but her vote still
counted.

Susan traveled all over the United States, working for **women's right** to **vote**. She also founded the National Woman **Suffrage** Association.

Susan worked all her life to get the vote for women. On her eighty-sixth birthday she said, "Failure is impossible!" She died on March 13, 1906. This was still fourteen years before the **law** allowed women to vote.

Part Two

This is a photograph of Susan B. Anthony when she was teaching. It shows us what she looked like.

Elizabeth Cady Stanton organized the first **women's rights** convention in 1848. This is a magazine picture of that convention.

Many women who worked for **equal rights** were treated badly. This cartoon makes fun of women working for equal rights.

AN AD-DRESS FOR THE CAUSE.

Susan B. Anthony started a newspaper to spread the word about **women's rights**. This is the front page of her paper. It was called *The Revolution*.

Susan B. Anthony and Elizabeth Cady Stanton became good friends when they met. This photograph shows Susan and Elizabeth reading a letter together.

> February 15. 1900.
>
> My dear friend
>
> Perfect ~~Political~~ equality
> of rights for women—
> civil and political — is
> to-day, and has been for
> the past half-century the
> one demand of
>
> Yours Sincerely
>
> Susan B. Anthony
>
> Rochester — N. Y.

This letter from Susan to Elizabeth talks about their work. In the letter, Susan says she wants "perfect" **equality**, not just the right to **vote**. She meant that she wanted men and women to be equal in everything.

In 1920, a new **law** gave women the right to **vote**. This law is called the "Susan B. Anthony **Amendment**." This photograph shows women celebrating the new law.

In 1978, the Susan B. Anthony silver dollar
was **minted** to honor this determined
woman who fought for **equal rights**. This
photograph shows what it looks like.

Glossary

This glossary explains difficult words, and helps you to say words which may be hard to say.

amendment Law changing the **Constitution of the United States**.

artifacts Objects made by people today or long ago. You say *AR tuh faks*.

Civil War War between the northern and southern states which began in 1861 and ended in 1865.

election day Day every four years on which Americans **vote** for a president.

equal/equality Everyone being the same.

equal rights Rules or laws which make sure everyone is treated the same.

laws Rules.

minted How a coin is made.

property Lands and buildings that can be owned.

Quaker Follower of the Quaker religion. Quakers are Christians.

slave Somebody who is owned by another person and must work for no pay.

suffrage Right to vote. You say *SUHfrij*.

United States Constitution Document that forms the basis for **laws** in the United States. You say *KON stih TOO shun*.

vote To say who you want to win.

weaving mill Factory for making cloth.

women's rights Rights of women to be treated equally to men.

women's rights movement Women and men working together to change **laws** which treat women unfairly.

Index

More Books to Read

Klingel, Cynthia and Dan Zadra. *Susan B. Anthony*. Mankato, Minn.: Creative Education, 1987.